Moonbeams in the Bitter Rain

What a privilege to enter Jayne's injured yet insightful world, 'her mind's pasture', through her poetry. Here we have a glimpse of her pain, rage and fear after the cruel legacy of a fateful moment in time. It could have been so easy for her to surrender to a suffering state of disability and yet in dreams and sleep she enters her own marvellous inner world. She sees the glory of the moon and sun, is inspired by birdsong and the sound of rain and wind, and she shows us an extraordinary ability to distil the essence of life to just a few gifted words. The emergent flower that Helen Sage writes of in *A Flower Between the Cracks* is beheld first-hand in this work. We are spellbound by the beauty of her soul.

David Lawry OAM (Co-founder TREENET, Founder of Avenues of Honour Project) and Julie Lawry (English teacher, New Arrivals Program. Thebarton Senior College, Adelaide)

As I ventured through *Moonbeams in the Bitter Rain*, I gained a glimpse of Jayne's extraordinary mind and how she encapsulates, both physically and spiritually, the effects of her life-changing event. The magical, mystical way her words reflect her personal journey of coming to terms with her new self and the rehabilitation process she endured took me to an emotional place, as if right alongside her. Jayne's poems, expressing her innermost conscious thoughts, are hauntingly honest, fragile yet brave, pure and simply beautifully written.

Sandi Sando, Coordinator Community Re-entry Program, University Practicum Supervisor and Tutor, Flinders University

Jayne and Keely (photo by Naomi Jellicoe)

Jayne Linke

Moonbeams
in the Bitter Rain

Acknowledgements

Some of these poems have been previously published:
'Daylight Painting' in *Positive Words for creative writers everywhere*,
Rainbow Press, Traralgon, Victoria, February 2007
and in *Poetry Matters*, Issue 22, November 2014
'Kookaburra Chorus' in The Friends of the Waite Arboretum
newsletter No. 52, Adelaide, 2007
'Muse Cruising' in *Beyond the Rainbow*, No. 35,
Mousetrap Media, Nimbin, 2008
'Walking' in *Artstate*, No. 14, Arts SA, Adelaide
and *Unruly Sun*, Friendly Street Poets 31
(in association with Wakefield Press, Adelaide), 2006
'Sunrise', 'Maniacal Moon', 'Brain Rape', 'Fear Factory',
'Resurrection', 'The Last Word', 'Kookaburra Chorus',
'Daylight Painting', 'Fable Label', 'Chastity Belt', 'Ochre Home',
'Muse Cruising', 'Winter Cherub', 'Highlighter Flight'
in *A Flower Between the Cracks*, Helen Sage, Affirm Press,
South Melbourne, 2013

'Ochre Home' shared first prize in the Literary Awards,
High Beam Disability Arts Festival, 2002.

Moonbeams in the Bitter Rain
ISBN 978 1 76041 322 4
Copyright © Jayne Linke 2017
Cover photo: Innes Linke

First published 2017 by
GINNINDERRA PRESS
PO Box 3461 Port Adelaide 5015 Australia
www.ginninderrapress.com.au

Contents

Foreword	9
Introduction	13
Brain Rape	17
Fear Factory	18
Hibernation	19
Solitude	20
Reflection	21
Maniacal Moon	22
Resurrection	23
The Last Word	24
Earthen Rebirth	25
Tempest	26
Gnosis	27
Fable-label	28
Chastity Belt	29
Beauty	30
Sale's Purple Haze	31
Walking	32
Dream Fields	33
Ochre Home	34
Elements at Play	35
La Nuit	36
Dream Steed	37
Sunrise	38
Salt Marsh Scamper	39
Muted Coot	40

Muse Cruising	41
Daylight Painting	42
Dream Slipstream	43
Highlighter Flight	44
Kookaburra Chorus	45
Winter Cherub	46
Seashore	47
Notes on the poems	49

For my mother and father, Helen and Innes,

and my twin sister Sarah –

this book is for you

Sarah and Jayne four years after Jayne's accident

Foreword

I met Jayne Linke some years ago in the company of her mother Helen during the spectacular jacaranda season in Adelaide. It was a clinical visit, and my first ever meeting with Jayne.

This was no ordinary consultation. Jayne wanted to scuba dive and needed a medical clearance to proceed. As she had substantial neuromuscular and movement control issues, I knew that they would pose quite a challenge to starting such lessons. Although somewhat taken aback, I asked myself and the Universe, 'Why not?'

And so – encouraged by Helen's calm counterpoint in her role as Jayne's carer – I began thinking aloud of the steps that would be needed, and in this gradual process of enquiry, the scuba plan unfolded and was indeed put in place.

It was years later that I received from Helen a gift copy of her memoir *A Flower between the Cracks*. This exquisitely written book tells the story of Jayne's devastating accident and its aftermath, of its impact upon Helen and her family, in Helen's own words as a grieving mother. Within the first two pages I was in tears, so movingly had Helen described her anguish in the earliest days and, later, months of Jayne's hospitalisation, when the lasting extent of her injuries was realised, although it was ultimately an uplifting story.

How poignant and beautiful now to be able to hear Jayne's own words in the form of these thirty-one impressionist poems. These are direct renditions of Jayne's recollections and perceptions of that same journey of recovery to which Helen bore witness and honoured in her memoir.

The earliest writings made by Jayne as she started to communicate in words and fragments were gathered up and cherished by Helen during that time and thereafter. As a faithful and loving amanuensis, she recorded them in their historical context. Jayne's writings are now presented as a cohesive whole.

We discover in the introduction how those early words began to emerge from the silence of coma and how encouraging they were to Jayne's loved ones. The writings gave them some insight into Jayne's inner world as she strove to make sense of the losses that she faced and move forward in recovery.

Jayne's experiences in hospital and during the slow process of re-enablement present us with stunning and original imagery. Her images are powerful and sometimes shocking, yet also luminous and lovely. In 'Hibernation': 'Ouch! I crouch and swerve from touch'. In 'Maniacal Moon': 'Gleaming and beaming overhead, alighting on the semi-dead. In 'Ochre Home': '… this ochre-silted golden filtered river sets me free.'

We then find another special page with concluding notes on Jayne's poetry, where her mother has correlated specific poems with particular milestones of Jayne's recovery pathway. This page appears just after the last amazingly delicate poem, 'Seashore'. Jayne often plays with the sound and feel of words, with pristine awareness of the ebb and flow of life: 'Saltwater's silken sleeve on sand, enchanting each and every man', creating a sense of reverence and stillness. Thus we are assured of the deep satisfaction and comfort that Jayne has found in the ways of nature.

This final commentary was very meaningful for me, as it enhanced my understanding of Jayne's clarity of perception and paid a wonderful tribute to the persona of the poet within the poems, through Helen's deeply felt love and appreciation of her daughter's qualities. Jayne's poems are truly meditative. They illuminate the resilience within that can grow to become the lifeline that draws us onward and upward despite profound loss. There is also a sense of timelessness within every single one of Jayne's treasured writings.

This scintillating collection presents Jayne's poems that capture vivid word pictures and stand alone as a set of vibrant, impressionistic pieces.

I believe that *Moonbeams in the Bitter Rain* by Jayne Linke and *A Flower Between the Cracks* by Helen Sage can be viewed as complementary pieces each to the other which further enhance the experience of Jayne's unique poetry for the reflective reader.

Dr Miranda Jelbart
Rehabilitation Physician
June 2016

Introduction

In 1999, when driving home from a university placement through a rogue corner in the Adelaide Hills, Jayne Linke, then an honours psychology student, sustained catastrophic injuries. She was just twenty-two years old. For nine weeks, she lay comatose in Flinders Medical Centre before awakening ever so gradually.

During six years of daily rehab, Jayne learned to breathe, eat and drink and eventually to speak and write again. However, Jayne's life remains very different, the ongoing impacts of her injuries requiring her to have a carer alongside every day to nurture, assist and support.

Throughout the early part of her post-accident journey, Jayne's poetry was a godsend to all those around her. Fine, spare and beautiful, each verse shed light upon her innermost world. As has been said of the poetry of Yevgeniy Yevtushenko, Jayne's verse carried 'the whole range of the human voice, shouts, whispers, conversation, moans, even silence'.

During rehab and through her vast losses, Jayne took her experiences one day at a time, first spelling then scribing thoughts: her fears, her strengths, her insights and wisdoms. Over her long years of partial recovery, Jayne's natural bent towards optimism, never far from the surface, eventually broke through to persist and prevail. How blessed are those close to her, to be so reassured, so inspired by her robust attitudes and writings.

Years on from her near death, rehab and recovery, Jayne's poetry attests to the remarkable adaptabilities of the human spirit for, though cloistered in her chair, she emanates agility and hope. Jayne's poems, so open, fresh and full of life, intrigue and captivate.

'You can muffle the drum, and you can loosen the strings of the lyre, but who shall command the skylark not to sing.'

Kahlil Gibran

Brain Rape

Surgeon inserts
a long hard probe.

Violation, for the best.
'No pain, no gain.'

'Please, come inside.
Do your worst!'

Fear Factory

Teeth clenched,
spasmodic clonus

shakes my stricken body,
as if a nameless fear hovers

…the future!

My wasted body lies
the object of benevolence.

Seaweed tentacles extend
over this reef of life

…sparkling, glowing.

Hibernation

'Ouch!' I crouch
& swerve from touch;

wary, wild, wolfish;
sleep my warm shield.

My blankets cover me
from harm or evil

as my soul wanders over hills
& gaze-length plains.

What awaits me?

Solitude

Solitude wraps me like a veil
over what is meant to be covert,
a hidden pain.

It's as if people think,
'If you don't mention it,
it will go away.'

People tread with such
excruciating caution.
They seem to think,

I'm FRAGILE…

'Handle with care'
becomes the
understatement of the year.

Reflection

My mind
is a nomad gypsy.

Cloudy fortune-teller's ball.

On the shelf,
ahead for me,

I see
masochy
&
parody.

Maniacal Moon

Cast your rune,
break the gloom,
maniacal moon.

Gleaming &
beaming overhead,
alighting on the semi-dead.

Sterile aroma
of folk under coma
takes me dolefully back –

But I'm NOT going there.
It isn't FAIR.
I've spent SOOO long in repair!

For me,
is it to be a life sentence
in the scalding clutches of Purgatory?

Resurrection

Red
raw
on the rack
– writhing wreck, in rack and ruin.
Paws pocked with pressure points,
criss-crossed
crazily.
Cruel
crucifixion!
Is it
my
time
to rise?

The Last Word

Some may hold the mistaken belief
that I should be sad – racked with grief.
But what overwhelms is a shield of RELIEF
'cos MEMORY, although a merciless tease,
acts as a mat beneath a trapeze.
Catching the acrobat of my mind,
she only leaves the note
unsigned.

Earthen Rebirth

My curled world
is no longer

an aggregate
of barbaric pain,

sadistic torture
& other noxious stimuli.

Joie de vivre
is a FREE, wild,

novel feeling,
startling in simplicity.

Light begins to penetrate
the boiling, seething void

of my unfurling world.
I've unrolled,

'Behold,

grass does grow greener
on the other side!'

Tempest

Rain,
thumping on corrugated iron,
croons a capella soundtrack.
Memory clouds those dark dayze…
sealed now in fog's haze,
mercifully
opaque!

Gnosis

A
mystical
pendulum,

my yoke
to the weight
of the world.

I have seen
the other side!

Something called me back
to finish this off;

the game
of life.

Fable-label

In the REAL world,
and is that a mirage?

Some folk will call it
'brain damage'.

But now they
MUST learn,

MIND & BODY
are on different planets;

a tight misshapen body
can NOT put the brain to sleep!

Am I now to find
that 'disabled' is a fable-label?

Chastity Belt

Earthen, unaffected,
demure allure – pure!

GET REAL!
What's the deal?

He kissed my paw;
I double took,

curtsied, scraped my jaw
off the floor.

FULLY caught on the back foot;
way off-guard!

Blessed unawares,
I regressed to a staggering virgin.

Earthbound eyes, streetwise;
afraid of failure

to match his pain
with my damaged brain.

Beauty

Beauty
is all around me.
I have only to pick up
my rose-coloured glasses,
sculling from them like a wino,
…but they leave a bitter
aftertaste.

Sale's Purple Haze

Amid the music sale's purple haze,
you meet my coolly wanton gaze,

…so straight and true.
I guess now, I'm thanking you

for treating me like a worthy, valid human being
and not some broken-down machine

as is, so much, a standard way
in what can be a cut-throat game!

So treat folk HUMAN, as you do,
it will, one day, come back to you.

Walking

Step…by step…by step…by step.
Slow…but it's progress.

Rain outside; rhythmic, driving,
placidly persistent,

> It's my melody
> for movement.

Dream Fields

I am owner and keeper of a priceless gift
and I may return here, in my mind's pasture,

for all daydreaming is gratis,
anyplace and anytime that I decide!

A moment to wallow inside the reviving breeze,
then let life's adventure trail-ride go on.

Ochre Home

Graceless and awkward,
Nature's sleight of hand,

you seem to be like me;
a waddling misfit on the land.

But at home on the lake you belong,
becoming demurely balanced and poised;

regal and grand,
gracefully in hand.

I think if you could talk to me,
you'd understand, you'd see –

like a cosy home, this ochre-silted
golden-filtered river sets me free.

Elements at Play

It's
as if
the earth

were sweating
in rivulets;

coursing down
the cliff face,

they trickle
thickly,

like true
tears
of
joy.

La Nuit

Je parlez
en mon coeur
c'est la nuit…
C'est mon ami, c'est belle beaucoup.

The Night

I speak
in my heart
it's the night…
It's my friend, it's very beautiful.

Dream Steed

I'm off for a ride
on my horse of the night.

Hop post and jump rail,
up hill and down dale.

Through field, over thicket;
a cheap freedom ticket.

I'm dreaming absurd –
I'm as free as a bird.

Sunrise

Sunshine
streaming in,
is dappled,

resembling the hide
of the RDA* horse
I ride.

Like a ray of sunshine
she warms
my heart,

thaws the frosty dew,
and looks like
gold to me.

* Riding for Disabled Association

Salt Marsh Scamper

I could run all day across the sand,
my feet are thudding and it makes an echo
in my mind, just like a hoofprint trail.

The sky meets the sea at the horizon;
I am riding through a blue
and yellow field of harmony.

Through my legs there is a
grasp of flickered white; the horse's loins.
Seagulls scatter the far reaches of my sight.

I pull him up, he drops his head.
No grass to eat here, he's just stretching.
So I take the cue and lie across his back.

Muted Coot

Tough & resolute
like grease-slicked jute,
a lonely coot among
the squabbling flock of ducks;

shining like a
dark soloist Druid in the park,
beneath his cloudy shroud
of subtle camouflage…

Oh I could be
like you;
a muted shooting
star!

Muse Cruising

I run my fingers through the sand;
they're splayed out like a comb.

Here in this space I feel my way,
afraid to call it home,

but it can be my holiday;
a place to slide and roam

and play among the ripples
and wallow in a poem.

Daylight Painting

So tender, yet the canvas
of today is stretched and waiting.

Will this morning bring to me
a mild Monet or a bold Van Gogh?

Morning sunshine thaws blue glass and the moon
has left her smudgy fingerprint on the window-pane.

I can only crouch and wait
for it'll happen this I know…

So let the precious day unfold for it can be
just like unwrapping any other gift!

Dream Slipstream

Easily I splash & wade
through slumber's soft, wild serenade.

My wake-up call – a perky brew,
the promised land he takes me to.

'Well, top o' the morning to you, my friend.
May sunrise bring some light to bend.'

My morning shooter soon kicks in;
I lie & dream in sleep-slipstream.

Highlighter Flight

In brilliant hues,
      they leave their bruise;

            the rainbow trail,
                a burning veil.

                      Come in to dock,
                        you livid flock.

                    You're nature's
              boldly sailing,

      wildly flailing,
bright highlighter flight!

Kookaburra Chorus

Raucous,
rolling
xylophone!

You
so relieve
the city drone.

In silent wonder,
I adore your chortle…

…as you pick the sonic bones away,
the wonder of a brand-new day uncurls.

You ring the day in truly new!

Bring to our ears,
the glory
of
your
warring,
morning chorus.

Winter Cherub

I am the moon shining in the bitter rain.
Chill breezes make me surge with joy.
When cold is king the pollen goes to sleep.
And I will frolic as a winter cherub.

Seashore

Salt water's silken sleeve on sand,
enchanting each & every man.

A whisper wind across my ear,
subdues away my fragile fear.

Hypnotic in its chill embrace,
o'er my cheek it casts a lace.

Roughly smooth, it heaves & sighs,
easy mantra-tantalise.

Notes on the poems

Jayne's poems give compelling record of her recovery. 'Fear Factory' refers to the caring hands of nurses during coma arousal, 'seaweed tentacles extend over this reef of life, sparkling, glowing'. 'Gnosis' – special knowledge of spiritual mysteries – alludes to her return from the edge, 'a mystical pendulum, my yoke to the weight of the world'. 'Earthen Rebirth' refers both to coma and new life, 'Light begins to penetrate the boiling, seething void of my unfurling world.' 'Maniacal Moon' inspired by the glare of an X-ray lamp, cries out, 'is it to be a life sentence in the scalding clutches of Purgatory?'

Jayne's early feelings of cruel sabotage are portrayed in poems such as 'Brain Rape' where, alluding to the brutality of enforced change, she pens, 'Surgeon inserts a long hard probe. Violation for the best…' And in 'Resurrection' 'red raw on the rack – writhing wreck, in rack and ruin.' While in 'Hibernation' she cries for space: 'I crouch and swerve from touch. Wary, wild, wolfish.'

Jayne's verse highlights a vibrant mind; a mind that yearns to be heeded. In 'Fable-label' she states firmly, 'mind and body are on different planets; a tight, misshapen body can NOT put the brain to sleep.' In 'Sales Purple Haze' she writes of her music shop man's friendly transaction, 'I'm thanking you, for treating me like a worthy, valid human being and not some broken down machine.'

At times, in a body severely maimed, Jayne questions

her future and her capacities. In 'Chastity Belt', unsure of both herself and the effect of her chair, she responds to a rehab flirtation, 'blessed unawares, I regressed to a staggering virgin, afraid of failure…to match his pain with my damaged brain.' And in 'Reflection' she muses, 'ahead for me I see masochy and parody.'

Yet, while awakening to severe disability and to arduous rehab, Jayne refuses to despair. Instead, her spirit permeates each page. In 'Winter Cherub' she writes, 'I am the moon shining in the bitter rain.' And in 'Dream Fields' comes a unique wisdom that humbles her reader: 'I am owner and keeper of a priceless gift…'

Throughout her writing, the solace of nature is a pervasive theme, such as in 'Ochre Home': 'this ochre-silted, golden filtered river sets me free.' And in 'Muse Cruising': 'here, in this space I feel my way, afraid to call it home. But it can be my holiday; a place to slide and roam.'

Gradually as Jayne reorients and ever so slowly adapts to her plight, she celebrates survival as in 'Earthen Rebirth': '*joie de vivre* is a free, wild feeling, startling in simplicity.' And in 'Daylight Painting' she sings, 'so let the precious day unfold for it can be just like unwrapping any other gift'.

Many years on from her near death and 'rebirth', Jayne grasps hold of life devoid of bitterness. Often her poems spellbind. Always they invigorate, reminding us of the extraordinary resilience of the human spirit.

www.ingramcontent.com/pod-product-compliance
Lightning Source LLC
Chambersburg PA
CBHW062205100526
44589CB00014B/1964